AQA PSYCHOLOGy A-LEVEL YEAR 2. FOUR WHOLE A STAR EXAM PAPERS. PAPERS 1 AND 2

Full mark answers to 4 Past Papers.

By Joseph Anthony Campbell

CONTENTS

Contents 1

Summary of the Examination Papers. 3

AQA A-Level Psychology (7182/1) 5

Paper 1..5

Introductory Topics in Psychology. 5

Specimen Material (First Set) 2017 5

Section A: Social Influence 6

Section B: Memory...10

Section C: Attachment 14

Section D: Psychopathology 18

AQA A-Level Psychology (7182/2)...23

Paper 2 23

Psychology in Context 23

Specimen Material (First Set) 2017 23

Section A: Approaches in Psychology 24

Section B: Biopsychology...28

Section C: Research Methods..32

AQA A-level Psychology (7182/1) 40

Paper 1 40

Introductory Topics in Psychology..40

2017 (Second Set) 40

Wednesday 7 June 2017 Afternoon 40

Time allowed: 2 hours 40

Section A: Social Influence..41

Section B: Memory 46

Section C: Attachment...50

Section D: Psychopathology 54

AQA A-level Psychology (7182/2) 58

Paper 2..58

Psychology in Context..58

2017 (Second Set)..58

Wednesday 14 June 2017 Afternoon 58

Time allowed: 2 hours..58

Section A: Approaches in Psychology 59

Section B: Biopsychology 63

Section C: Research Methods 67

Assessment Objectives. 75
Timings. 77
Approximate Word Count Per Mark in Psychology. 79
Author's Note. 82
About the Author. 83

SUMMARY OF THE EXAMINATION PAPERS.

The examinations are linear i.e., they are all done at the end of each year.

There are **2** examination papers for Psychology AS level.

There are **3** examination papers for Psychology A level.

(I have written further books to help you with the AS level and Paper 3 of the A level and I have provided details of the AS level Psychology papers and the Paper 3 A level topics in those Psychology books).

In this book, we are concerned with Paper 1 and Paper 2 of the A level examinations which are completed at the end of your 'A' levels (usually the end of Year 2).

Paper **1** is divided into **4** sections:

Section A - Social Influence

Section B – Memory

Section C – Attachment

Section D - Psychopathology

Each section is worth 24 marks and the paper has a total of 96 marks. There is 2 hours (120 minutes) for the exam (unless you have extra time).

Paper **2** is divided into **3** sections:

Section A – Approaches in Psychology

Section B – Psychopathology

Section C – Research Methods

Section A and B are worth 24 marks and Section C is worth 48 marks. The paper has a total of 96 marks. There is 2 hours (120 minutes) for the exam (unless you have extra time).

Each Paper is worth one third of your total A level Psychology mark.

The exam structure is complicated. In each section there will be multiple choice questions, short answer questions and at least one extended writing question. This is why the examples in this book are particularly useful as you will need to familiarise yourself with these types of questions and their structure for each examination. They range from 1 to 16 marks per question.

AQA A-LEVEL PSYCHOLOGY (7182/1)
PAPER 1
INTRODUCTORY TOPICS IN PSYCHOLOGY.
SPECIMEN MATERIAL (FIRST SET) 2017

SECTION A: SOCIAL INFLUENCE

Answer __all__ questions in this section (24 marks and 30 minutes for each section on Paper 1)

0 1 Which of the following terms best matches the statements below? Choose __one__ term that matches __each__ statement and write A, B, C, D or E in the box next to it. Use each letter once only.

A Identification
B Informational social influence
C Normative social influence
D Compliance
E Internalisation

[4 marks] (5 minutes) (AO1 = 4)

Publicly changing behaviour whilst maintaining a different private view. [1 mark]

D

Group pressure leading to a desire to fit in with the group. [1 mark]

C

When a person lacks knowledge of how to behave and looks to the group for guidance. [1 mark]

B

Conforming to the behaviour of a role model. [1 mark]

A

0 2 Briefly outline <u>and</u> evaluate the findings of any <u>one</u> study of social influence.

[4 marks] (5 minutes) (AO1 = 2; AO3 = 2) (100 words maximum)

Asch placed male participants in an unambiguous situation where the majority of participants conformed at least once when confederates gave the same wrong answer to a question comparing line lengths across various trials. 75% of participants conformed at least once across 18 trials.

(AO1=2)

The study lacks ecological validity however, as whether the participants were right or wrong did not really matter to the participants; they may have been less likely to conform if their answers had real-life consequences. Also, in terms of ethics, the participants were deceived as to the true nature of the study.

(AO3=2)

(95 words)

0 3 Read the item and then answer the question that follows.

Two psychology students were discussing the topic of social influence.

'I find it fascinating how some people are able to resist social influence', said Jack. 'It must be the result of having a confident personality.'

'I disagree', replied Sarah. 'I think resisting social influence depends much more on the presence of others.'

Discuss two explanations of resistance to social influence. As part of your discussion, refer to the views expressed by Jack and Sarah in the conversation above.

[16 marks] (20 minutes) (AO1 = 6; AO2 = 4; AO3 = 6) (400 words maximum)

One explanation of resistance to social influence is that of social support, a situational factor. Sarah states that resistance depends on 'the presence of others' and Milgram found that participants are less likely to obey authority if there were other dissenting confederates present. Asch found similar results in variations of his experiment on conformity in an unambiguous situation when he tested the effect of the participant having a supporter in the group i.e., one of the confederates agreed with the participant. Having a fellow dissenter who disagreed with the majority broke the unanimity of the group. This made it easier for the participant to resist the pressure to conform and the rate of conformity fell to 5.5%. This finding is reflected in Sarah's comment that 'social influence depends much more on the presence of others.'

Jack however suggests that dispositional factors in resisting social influence are more important. Another explanation of resistance is that of 'locus of control'. Jack states that '...how some people are able to resist social influence...must be the result of having a confident personality'. If someone has an internal locus of control, they are more likely to accept personal responsibility for their own actions. They are therefore less likely to obey authoritative demands that are against both their morals and views. If someone has an external locus of control, they are less likely to accept personal responsibility for their actions and are therefore more likely to feel helpless and obedient when confronted with a perceived authority figure. This explanation of resistance to social influence provides an alternative, viable explanation through a dispositional factor as to why people would resist social influence.

However as to the psychological experiments that have provided these two explanations of resistance to social influence, both Asch and Milgram's experiments have been criticised for the deceptive elements of their studies. Asch and Milgram' participants encounter the ethical issue of deception as Asch's participants believed that they were taking part in a study to determine line lengths whilst Milgram's participants believed that the experiment was based on the effects of punishment on learning and that they were actually providing electric shocks to participants. The experiments could have had a long-term impact on the participants and both experiments could therefore lack validity and be criticised for their levels of ecological validity due to the fact that they were both artificial laboratory experiments.

(397 words)

SECTION B: MEMORY

Answer <u>all</u> questions in this section (24 marks and 30 minutes for each section on Paper 1)

Read the item and then answer the questions that follow.

An experiment was carried out to test the effects of learning similar and dissimilar information on participants' ability to remember.

In <u>Stage 1</u> of the experiment, 10 participants in <u>Group A</u>, the 'similar' condition, were given a list of 20 place names in the UK. They were given two minutes to learn the list. 10 different participants in <u>Group B</u>, the 'dissimilar' condition, were given the same list of 20 place names in the UK. They were also given two minutes to learn the list.

In <u>Stage 2</u> of the experiment, participants in <u>Group A</u> were given a different list of 20 more place names in the UK, and were given a further two minutes to learn it. Participants in <u>Group B</u> were given a list of 20 boys' names, and were given a further two minutes to learn it.

In <u>Stage 3</u> of the experiment, all participants were given five minutes to recall as many of the 20 place names in the UK, from the list in <u>Stage 1</u>, as they could. The raw data from the two groups is below.

Table 1: Number of place names recalled from the list in Stage 1.

Group A	*Group B*
5	11
6	10
4	11
7	13
8	12
4	14
5	15
4	11
6	14
7	14

0 4-0 1 What is the most appropriate measure of central tendency for calculating the average of the scores, from Table 1, in each of the two groups? Justify your answer.

[2 marks] (2.5 minutes) (AO2 = 2) (50 words maximum)

The mean is the appropriate measure of central tendency for calculating the average of the scores. The mean is the most sensitive method as it takes all the scores in each data set into account.

(35 words)

0 4-0 2 Calculate the measure of central tendency you have identified in your answer to question 04.0 1 for Group A and Group B. Show your calculations for each group.

[4 marks] (5 minutes) (AO2 = 4)

5+6+4+7+8+4+5+4+6+7=56/10= 5.6 = Group A mean

11+10+11+13+12+14+15+11+14+14=125/10= 12.5 = Group B mean

0 4-0 3 In <u>Stage 3</u> of the experiment, several participants in <u>Group A</u>, the 'similar' condition, recalled words from the <u>Stage 2</u> list rather than the <u>Stage 1</u> list.

Use your knowledge of forgetting to explain why this may have occurred.

[2 marks] (2.5 minutes) (AO2 = 2) (50 words maximum)

The information presented in Stage 1 and Stage 2 was similar and the new information disrupted/interfered with the recall of previous information. This is called retroactive interference.

(27 words)

0 5 Describe <u>and</u> evaluate the working memory model of memory.

[16 marks] (20 minutes) (AO1 = 6; AO3 = 10) (400 words maximum)

The working memory model (WMM) was created by Baddeley and Hitch in 1974 and the model proposed that short term memory was comprised of three different stores; the phonological loop, the episodic buffer and the visuo-spatial sketchpad. The central executive receives all of the information that is paid attention to (attentional focus) and directs the information to one of the three slave systems according to its type. Speech-based information is directed to the phonological loop; visual and spatial information is directed towards the visuo-spatial sketchpad and the episodic buffer (2000) stores information from the other two slave systems and integrates the information together to form episodes along with information from long term memory (LTM) in order to make complete scenes or form 'episodes. All of the slave systems have limited capacity and duration and therefore in order to store information for a long time, information must be passed on to the long-term memory.

The working memory model is supported by evidence such as the case study of KF by Shallice and Washington (1974). KF sustained brain damage in a motorbike accident and had problems with certain areas of short-term memory. KF could recall and process visual information but had trouble recalling words verbally. This suggests that he had an impaired articulatory loop but an intact visuo-spatial sketchpad. KF's condition could not be explained by the multi-store model of memory (MSM) which delineates short term memory as one store and in the case of KF it instead supports the working memory model's theory that short-term memory is made up of multiple stores and an active processor unlike the multi-store model of memory which contains a discrete store only.

The working memory model also does not place as much emphasis on rehearsal as the multi-store model. Rehearsal is only one possible process in the working memory model which helps to explain how information enters the long-term memory after little or no rehearsal. This means that the working memory model allows for other explanations on processes rather than one finite explanation as provided by the multi-store model.

However, some psychologists argue that the central executive is too vague and simplistic in its description; it is merely described as 'attention' in the working memory model. The central executive concept is also not supported as it is extremely difficult to design tasks to test it and therefore there is little empirical evidence for its existence.

(400 words)

SECTION C: ATTACHMENT

Answer <u>all</u> questions in this section (24 marks and 30 minutes for each section on Paper 1)

06 Name <u>three</u> stages in the development of attachments identified by Schaffer.

[3 marks] (3.75 minutes) (AO1 = 3)

1 Pre-attachment (Asocial)
2 Indiscriminate (Multiple)
3 Discriminate (Single)

07 Read the item and then answer the question that follows.

A nursery school worker and her manager were chatting at the end of the day.

'How did the new toddlers settle in today?' asked the manager.

'They behaved very differently', replied the nursery school worker. 'Max was distressed when his mother left but was happy to see her at the end of the day.'

'Jessica arrived clinging to her mother and I could not calm her down when her mother left.'

'*William barely seemed to notice when his mother left and did not even look up when she returned to collect him.*'

Name the attachment type demonstrated by <u>*each*</u> *of the children in the conversation above by writing the attachment type next to the name below.*

[3 marks] (3.75 minutes) (AO2 = 3)

Max   Secure

Jessica   Insecure – resistant

William   Insecure – avoidant

0 8 Briefly evaluate learning theory as an explanation of attachment.

[4 marks] (5 minutes) (AO3 = 4) (100 words maximum)

Support for learning theory is derived from scientific research involving research on animals. This is a limitation because it presents the problem of anthropomorphic extrapolation because it is not possible to fully extrapolate from animals to humans as humans and animals are inherently different. It is also difficult to tell in learning theory if an association has taken place and if it ever will take place when studying babies in their early months. For example, Schaffer and Emerson (1964) found that many babies did not have their mother as the primary attachment figure despite the mother being the primary caregiver.

(100 words)

0 9 Read the item and then answer the question that follows.

A group of researchers used 'event sampling' to observe children's friendships over a period of three weeks at break times and lunchtimes during the school day.

Explain what is meant by 'event sampling'.

[2 marks] (2.5 minutes) (AO1 = 2) (50 words maximum)

'Event sampling' is when researchers comprise a list of events they want to study (e.g., holding hands, speaking aloud) and compile a period of time in which to record said events (e.g., 5 hourly periods). The researchers then record the events that occur in the period of time previously designated.

(50 words)

1 0 The investigation in <u>*question 09*</u> *is an example of a 'naturalistic observation'. Briefly discuss how observational research might be improved by conducting observations in a controlled environment.*

[4 marks] (5 minutes) (AO3 = 4) (100 words maximum)

Controlled environments such as laboratory experiments offer a strong level of control of extraneous variables during observational research. Extraneous variables can interfere or affect the results of the observational research. The removal or minimising of said extraneous variables makes it easier to both establish a causal relationship between the independent and dependent variable and for a later researcher to conduct the same experiment/observation and replicate the same results. This increases both the reliability and the validity of the observational research which could be improved by conducting observations in a controlled environment.

(91 words)

11 Discuss research into the influence of early attachment on adult relationships.

[8 marks] (10 minutes) (AO1 = 4; AO3 = 4) (200 words maximum)

Hazan and Shaver (1987) conducted a 'love quiz' in a local newspaper. The quiz assessed the attachment type (secure, insecure resistant or insecure avoidant) between participants and their parents. The other section assessed their current beliefs about romantic love. The first 620 responses were analysed and secure children tended to have fully functional, trusting relationships; insecure resistant children were more likely to be extremely worried that they were not loved in their relationships and insecure avoidant children tended to fear intimacy. This provides support for Bowlby's theory that adult relationships are influenced by early attachment.

However, Freud and Dann (1951) provided evidence that those early attachments may not have as large an effect on adult relationships as Hazan and Shaver's (1987) results implied. They studied 6 children who were orphaned during World War Two and raised in a deportation camp. They were unable to form any adult attachments. However, when the children grew up, they developed average intelligence and were able to form fully functioning relationships. Freud and Dann concluded that this was because they had formed attachments amongst themselves as children. This offers an alternative interpretation of a viable early attachment and its influence on later adult relationships.

(199 words)

SECTION D: PSYCHOPATHOLOGY

Answer <u>all</u> questions in this section (24 marks and 30 minutes for each section on Paper 1)

1 2 Which <u>two</u> of the following are examples of Jahoda's criteria for 'ideal mental health'? Shade <u>two</u> boxes only. For each answer completely fill in the circle alongside the appropriate answer.

[2 marks] (2.5 minutes) (AO1 = 2)

A Dependence on others
B Environmental mastery SHADE THIS BOX
C Lack of inhibition
D Maladaptiveness
E Resistance to stress SHADE THIS BOX

1 3 Read the item and then answer the question that follows.

The following article appeared in a magazine:

<u>*Hoarding disorder – A 'new' mental illness*</u>

Most of us are able to throw away the things we don't need on a daily basis. Approximately 1 in 1000 people, however, suffer from hoarding disorder, defined as 'a difficulty parting with items and possessions, which leads to severe anxiety and extreme clutter that affects living or work spaces'.

Apart from 'deviation from ideal mental health', outline <u>three</u> definitions of abnormality. Refer to the article above in your answer.

[6 marks] (7.5 minutes) (AO1 = 3; AO2 = 3) (150 words maximum)

One definition of abnormality is a deviation from statistical norms. Behaviour that is rare statistically is considered abnormal within this approach (people on the tail ends of a bell curve graph are statistically rare and therefore abnormal). People with 'hoarding disorder' are '1 in 1000 people', they are therefore statistically rare and abnormal.

Another definition of abnormality is an individual being unable to function adequately. Criteria for diagnosis include dysfunctional behaviour (behaviour which contrasts with the cultures accepted and expected behaviour) and personal distress (the individual is excessively emotional). In this case, the 'hoarding disorder' is causing the sufferers, 'severe anxiety'.

Deviation from social norms is a third definition of abnormality. This outlines an individual who contrasts with the expected and accepted behaviours of their society (the social norms). As the article states 'Most of us are able to throw away the things we don't need on a daily basis'.

(150 words)

1 4 Read the item and then answer the question that follows.

Kirsty is in her twenties and has had a phobia of balloons since one burst near her face when she was a little girl. Loud noises such as 'banging' and 'popping' cause Kirsty extreme anxiety, and she avoids situations such as birthday parties and weddings, where there might be balloons.

Suggest how the behavioural approach might be used to explain Kirsty's phobia of balloons.

[4 marks] (5 minutes) (AO2 = 4) (100 words maximum)

The behavioural approach may explain Kirsty's phobia of balloons as a product of classical conditioning i.e., Kirsty has learnt to associate balloons with fear. This means that a neutral stimulus (NS) (a balloon) has been presented with an unconditioned stimulus (UCS–loud noise) and produced an unconditioned response (UCR–fear). In this way balloons inspire and cause a response of fear in Kirsty. This fear has been maintained through operant conditioning as Kirsty's avoidance of situations where there might be balloons has prevented this conditioned anxiety and fear (CR–fear) from occurring (negative reinforcement). Thus, she may continually repeat this avoidant behaviour.

(99 words)

1 5 Read the item and then answer the questions that follow.

Twenty depressed patients were treated using cognitive behavioural therapy. Over the course of the six-week treatment, each patient's mood was monitored every week using a self-report mood scale (where a score of 20 = extremely positive mood and a score of 0 = extremely negative mood). Each week they also completed a quality of sleep questionnaire which was scored from 10 = excellent sleep to 0 = very poor sleep.

At the end of the study the researchers correlated each patient's final mood score with his or her final sleep score.

1 5-0 2 Outline <u>one</u> way in which the researchers should have dealt with ethical issues in this study.

[2 marks] (2.5 minutes) (AO3 = 2) (50 words maximum)

The researchers should have constantly offered or made the participants aware of the right for them to withdraw from the study. This would prevent participant discomfort and distress.

(28 words)

1 5-0 3 The sleep questionnaire used by the researchers had not been checked to see whether or not it was a reliable measure of sleep quality.

Explain how this study could be modified by checking the sleep questionnaire for test-retest reliability.

[4 marks] (5 minutes) (AO3 = 4) (100 words maximum)

This would be achieved by modifying the sleep questionnaire for test-retest reliability. Firstly, the participants would complete the sleep questionnaire more than once. The scores would then be correlated from each questionnaire. A scatter graph would also be used and on one axis the first tests results and, on another axis, the later test's results. This would then be assessed using a Spearman's Rho test and the reliability is then determined by comparing the correlation with the statistical table. It would be expected to display a strong, positive correlation between the two sets of scores.

(95 words)

1 6 Outline cognitive behaviour therapy as a treatment for depression.

[4 marks] (5 minutes) (AO1 = 4) (100 words maximum)

Cognitive behavioural therapy (CBT) attempts to identify and rectify the patient's faulty cognitions. There are many ways that the therapist and patient can do this. The therapist tries to help the client discern that these cognitions are faulty by questioning them and focusing upon the clients' successes in life. The client may be encouraged to keep a diary to help them become more aware of their thoughts and feelings. The therapy aims to mostly focus on what the client's personal situation is but the therapist may also draw on the client's past experiences.

(93 words)

AQA A-LEVEL PSYCHOLOGY (7182/2)
PAPER 2
PSYCHOLOGY IN CONTEXT
SPECIMEN MATERIAL (FIRST SET) 2017

SECTION A: APPROACHES IN PSYCHOLOGY

Answer __all__ questions in this section (24 marks and 30 minutes for this section)

0 1 Which __one__ of the following statements is __false__? Shade __one__ box only.

[1 mark] (1.25 minutes) (AO1 = 1)

A Repression can lead to unpleasant memories causing distress
B Repression causes people to have difficulty accessing unpleasant memories
C Repression involves people choosing to forget unpleasant memories   SHADE THIS BOX
D Repression involves unpleasant memories being kept from conscious awareness

0 1-0 2 Which __one__ of the following statements is __false__? Shade __one__ box only.

[1 mark] (1.25 minutes) (AO1 = 1)

A The Id is responsible for pleasure-seeking behaviour
B The Id is responsible for unreasonable behaviour
C The Superego is responsible for bad behaviour   SHADE THIS BOX
D The Superego is responsible for guilty feelings

0 2 Read the item and then answer the question that follows.

In a laboratory study of problem-solving, cognitive psychologists asked participants to solve problems presented in different colours of ink. They found that it took longer to solve problems presented in green ink, than it did to solve problems presented in other colours. They inferred that the mental processing of problems is made more difficult when a problem is presented in green ink.

Explain what is meant by 'inference' in relation to this study.

[2 marks] (2.5 minutes) (AO2 = 2) (50 words maximum)

Inference refers to assumptions made about mental processes that are not directly supported by evidence. In this context, the psychologists are inferring that because the green ink questions seemingly made the participants solve the problems at a slower rate that they then had more difficulty actually mentally processing the problems.

(50 words)

0 3 Read the item and then answer the question that follows.

Dominic is unhappy and lacks confidence. He also thinks he is not very good-looking and not very clever. He goes to a counselling therapist for help. The therapist suggests that Dominic lacks congruence.

Outline what is meant by 'congruence'. Explain <u>one</u> way in which Dominic might achieve 'congruence'.

[4 marks] (5 minutes) (AO1 = 2; AO2 = 2) (100 words maximum)

Congruence is the difference between the self as known to the individual and the self the person aspires to become. The therapist could endeavour to bridge the gap between the two incongruent aspects of this self for Dominic by helping him to be able to assess himself more accurately. Through the therapist offering Dominic unconditional positive regard (UPR), Dominic could achieve a more realistic view of himself.

(67 words)

0 4 Discuss the contribution of behaviourist psychologists such as Pavlov and Skinner to our understanding of human behaviour.

[16 marks] (20 minutes) (AO1 = 6; AO3 = 10) (400 words maximum)

Ivan Pavlov carried out an experiment whereby he rang a bell and then provided dogs with food immediately afterwards. The dogs began to associate the bell with food through repetition and soon the bell alone caused salivation. The food was an unconditioned stimulus that produced an unconditioned response (salivation). When the unconditioned stimulus was repeatedly presented with a neutral stimulus (the bell), it was associated with the unconditioned stimulus (the food) and produced a now conditioned response (salivation) and thus became a conditioned stimulus. Pavlov labelled this classical conditioning and it later became known as Pavlovian conditioning.

B.F. Skinner studied how animals and by extension, humans, learn from the consequences of their actions – in particular through positive and negative reinforcement. Positive reinforcement is when something desirable is obtained through the subject partaking in a particular behaviour and Skinner's experiments on rats display this as rats were conditioned to press a lever because it provided them with food, which was desirable. Negative reinforcement describes an undesirable experience or item being removed as a consequence of a particular behaviour and the rats also learnt to press a lever to prevent an electric shock. Skinner labelled this as operant conditioning.

However, although conditioning is supported by evidence, it cannot explain all behaviour. Animals and humans can also learn through observation as demonstrated by the social learning theory. This means that Skinner and Pavlov's theories into conditioning cannot be used on their own to explain all behaviour.

Both Pavlov and Skinner's experiments and much behaviourist evidence relies on animal research. This means that there is a problem of anthropomorphic extrapolation as humans and animals are inherently different in both morals and physicality. Therefore, there is a problem of relating animal studies to humans. Behaviourists seemingly ignore genetic factors also which can impact what different species can learn through conditioning.

Behaviourists also fail to take into account abstract concepts such as morals and also state the 'mind' is irrelevant. Both Skinner and Pavlov fail to outline cognitive processes that take place during conditioning and therefore provide an incomplete explanation of behaviour. It has been applied to classrooms in education and various modes of therapy however and applicability has been found in relation to the real world and it has been useful in understanding certain aspects of human behaviour.

(383 words)

SECTION B: BIOPSYCHOLOGY

*Answer **all** questions in this section (24 marks and 30 minutes for this section)*

0 6 The electroencephalogram (EEG) and event-related potentials (ERPs) both involve recording the electrical activity of the brain.

*Outline **one** difference between the EEG and ERPs.*

[2 marks] (2.5 minutes) (AO2 = 2) (50 words maximum)

EEG's show the overall electrical activity in the brain, meaning that it is often used to study sleep patterns.

ERP'S, however, display changes in EEG wave patterns in response to a stimulus, to link certain stimuli to certain responses.

(39 words)

0 7 Read the item and then answer the question that follows.

Sam is a police officer. She has just started working the night shift and after a week, she finds that she has difficulty sleeping during the day and is becoming tense and irritable. Sam is also worried that she is less alert during the night shift itself.

Using your knowledge of endogenous pacemakers and exogenous zeitgebers, explain Sam's experiences.

[4 marks] (5 minutes) (AO2 = 4) (100 words maximum)

Due to the fact that Sam has been on the night shift for a week her endogenous pacemaker or internal biological clock is out of sync with the exogenous zeitgeber of light. This is because she has to remain awake at night when it is dark and sleep during the day when it is light. This disruption in her sleep-wake cycle has been linked to the problem Sam is experiencing such as difficulty in sleeping and therefore feeling tense and irritable.

(81 words)

0 8 The human female menstrual cycle is an example of <u>one</u> type of biological rhythm; it is called a:

A circadian rhythm
B infradian rhythm
C ultradian rhythm

[1 mark] (1.25 minutes) (AO1 = 1)

B

0 9 Outline the structures and processes involved in synaptic transmission.

[6 marks] (7.5 minutes) (AO1 = 6) (150 words maximum)

When an electrical impulse reaches the end of a neuron, neurotransmitters are released into the synaptic cleft, which diffuse to the postsynaptic membrane. These neurotransmitters might trigger an electric pulse down the postsynaptic membrane therefore continuing through to the synaptic cleft. After the neurotransmitters trigger the electric pulse they are reabsorbed by the presynaptic neuron or broken down by enzymes.

Synaptic transmission occurs at the junction between two neurons. The receptors are on the postsynaptic membranes, which means that the impulses are unidirectional. Excitatory neurotransmitters (e.g., Acetylcholine) make it more likely that an electrical impulse in the postsynaptic neuron will be triggered. Inhibitory neurotransmitters such as gamma–Aminobutyric acid (GABA) make it less likely that an electrical impulse will be triggered in the postsynaptic neuron.

(124 words)

1 0 Split brain patients show unusual behaviour when tested in experiments. Briefly explain how unusual behaviour in split brain patients could be tested in an experiment.

[2 marks] (2.5 minutes) (AO2 = 2) (50 words maximum)

Participants who have had split brain surgery could split their visual field by covering one of their eyes in two conditions in a repeated measures experiment and when shown a word or a picture they could report or attempt to draw what they see.

(44 words)

1 1 Briefly evaluate research using split brain patients to investigate hemispheric lateralisation of function.

[4 marks] (5 minutes) (AO3 = 4) (100 words maximum)

Results found in split brain research cannot always be accurately generalised in order to create nomothetic theories due to their small sample size (e.g., Sperry used only 11 participants). Therefore, the findings do not allow for anomalies and have little practical use. Also, the findings of split-brain patients whom had had drug treatment were compared to an epileptic control group that had not experienced medical (drug) treatment or experienced epilepsy. Therefore, you cannot establish causal relationships when investigating hemispheric lateralisation of function between both splitting the brain and impaired function as impaired function may be due to the medication beforehand.

(100 words)

SECTION C: RESEARCH METHODS

Answer __all__ questions in this section (48 marks and 60 minutes for this section)

Read the item and then answer the questions that follow.

A psychologist wanted to see if verbal fluency is affected by whether people think they are presenting information to a small group of people or to a large group of people.

The psychologist needed a stratified sample of 20 people. She obtained the sample from a company employing 60 men and 40 women.

The participants were told that they would be placed in a booth where they would read out an article about the life of a famous author to an audience. Participants were also told that the audience would not be present, but would only be able to hear them and would not be able to interact with them.

There were two conditions in the study, __Condition A__ and __Condition B__.

__Condition A__: 10 participants were told the audience consisted of 5 listeners.
__Condition B__: the other 10 participants were told the audience consisted of 100 listeners.

Each participant completed the study individually. The psychologist recorded each presentation and then counted the number of verbal errors made by each participant.

1 2 Identify the dependent variable in this study.

[2 marks] (2.5 minutes) (AO2 = 2) (50 words maximum)

The dependent variable is the verbal fluency of the participants, which could be measured by the number of verbal errors they make.

(22 words)

1 3 Write a suitable hypothesis for this study.

[3 marks] (3.75 minutes) (AO2 = 3) (75 words maximum)

There is no difference in the number of verbal errors made by participants who believe they are reading to a small audience (5 listeners) and by participants who believe they are reading to a large audience (100 listeners).

(38 words)

1 4 Identify one extraneous variable that the psychologist should have controlled in the study and explain why it should have been controlled.

[3 marks] (3.75 minutes) (AO2 = 3) (75 words maximum)

It would be important to control the participant's level of familiarity with the famous author as increased levels of familiarity could decrease the number of verbal errors. This uncontrolled participant variable could affect the dependent variable (DV –verbal error rate) rather than the independent variable.

(45 words)

1 5 Explain <u>one</u> advantage of using a stratified sample of participants in this study.

[2 marks] (2.5 minutes) (AO2 = 2) (50 words maximum)

Stratified sampling can produce a representative sample of the group you are attempting to generalise the results to. This means that the results may have a higher level of validity when generalising to the general population as different genders male/female are represented in this study sample in the correct proportions.

(50 words)

1 6 Explain how the psychologist would have obtained the male participants for her stratified sample. Show your calculations.

[3 marks] (3.75 minutes) (AO2 = 3) (75 words maximum)

60% of the 20 participants should be male therefore: (60/100 x 20 = 12.)
12 participants should be male.
Place the names of 60 males written on a piece of paper in a hat and pick names from the hat until you have withdrawn 12 names. These 12 names are the men that will be used in the sample. Then determine the proportion of males needed to mirror the number of males in the target population as follows i.e., 60%.

(75 words)

1 7 The psychologist wanted to randomly allocate the 20 people in her stratified sample to the two conditions. She needed an equal number of males in each condition and an equal number of females in each condition. Explain how she would have done this.

[4 marks] (5 minutes) (AO2 = 4) (100 words maximum)

Firstly, the psychologist must write down all the names of the females on slips of paper and put them in a hat. Then the psychologist must randomly withdraw 4 names and put them in condition 1 and then withdraw 4 names and put them in condition 2. The psychologist then must write down all the names of the males on slips of paper and put them in a different hat and withdraw 6 names out of the hat. These will be the participants in condition 1. Then the psychologist must withdraw another 6 names and put them in condition 2.

(100 words)

1 8 Read the item and then answer the questions that follow.

The results of the study are given in Table 1.

Table 1: Mean number of verbal errors and standard deviations for both conditions

Condition A (believed audience of 5 listeners) Condition B (believed audience of 100 listeners)

	Condition A	Condition B
Mean	11.1	17.2
Standard deviation	1.30	3.54

What conclusions might the psychologist draw from the data in Table 1? Refer to the means and standard deviations in your answer.

[6 marks] (7.5 minutes) (AO2 = 2; AO3 = 4) (150 words maximum)

Firstly, the psychologist might conclude that more verbal errors are made when the person believes that they are presenting and reading to a large audience of 100 listeners than if they believe that they are reading to a small audience of 5 listeners. This conclusion is supported by the results of the mean as those in Condition B (believed an audience of 100 listeners) made an average of 17.2 verbal errors whereas those in Condition A (believed an audience of 5 listeners) made an average of 11.1 verbal errors. The psychologist might also conclude that the differences in participants public speaking skills and anxiety levels became more apparent when participants believed that they were presenting to a larger audience as the standard deviation was larger (3.54) in Condition B (believed an audience of 100 listeners) compared to Condition A (believed an audience of 5 listeners) (1.30).

(146 words)

1 9 Read the item and then answer the question that follows.

The psychologist had initially intended to use the range as a measure of dispersion in this study but found that one person in <u>Condition A</u> had made an exceptionally low number of verbal errors.

Explain how using the standard deviation rather than the range in this situation, would improve the study.

[3 marks] (3.75 minutes) (AO3 = 3) (75 words maximum)

The range can be easily affected by one anomalous result meaning that the range is easily affected by errors. In contrast, standard deviation measures the average distance of the scores from the mean not just the difference between the highest verbal error score and the lowest verbal error score and is therefore less easily distorted by a single anomalous or extreme score.

(62 words)

2 0 Name an appropriate statistical test that could be used to analyse the number of verbal errors in Table 1. Explain why the test you have chosen would be a suitable test in this case.

[4 marks] (5 minutes) (AO2 = 4) (100 words maximum)

An unrelated t – test could be used if we record results as interval data (i.e., one verbal error is recorded in the same fashion as another verbal error). The study is also an independent groups design and the psychologist is looking for a difference between the two conditions. All of these factors suggest that the unrelated t-test could be used.

(60 words)

2 1 The psychologist found the results were significant at p<0.05. What is meant by 'the results were significant at p <0.05'?

[2 marks] (2.5 minutes) (AO1 = 2) (50 words maximum)

This means that the researchers would have a 95% confidence level that the results are significant (i.e., the change in the independent variable is the cause of a change in the dependent variable).

(33 words)

2 2 Briefly explain <u>one</u> method the psychologist could use to check the validity of the data she collected in this study.

[2 marks] (2.5 minutes) (AO2 = 2) (50 words maximum)

They would make the participants take part in a different, established verbal fluency test and check to see that the results from both tests are consistent with one another and positively correlated (concurrent validity).

(34 words)

2 3 Briefly explain <u>one</u> reason why it is important for research to undergo a peer review process.

[2 marks] (2.5 minutes) (AO3 = 2) (50 words maximum)

The peers can check to make sure that not only are the researchers results valid but that the researcher's conclusion/s are supported by their results. This would ensure that the research is less likely to contain any errors when published as it has been independently, objectively scrutinised by peers.

(49 words)

2 4 Read the item and then answer the question that follows.

"The psychologist focused on fluency in spoken communication in her study. Other research has investigated sex differences in non-verbal behaviours such as body language and gestures."

Design an observation study to investigate sex differences in non-verbal behaviour of males and females when they are giving a presentation to an audience.

In your answer you should provide details of:

• the task for the participants
• the behavioural categories to be used and how the data will be recorded
• how reliability of the data collection might be established
• ethical issues to be considered.

[12 marks] (15 minutes) (AO2 = 12) (300 words maximum)

The participants should give an approximately 10-minute individual presentation to an audience from a script such as 'a list of favourite hobbies' that the psychologists have given them 20 minutes before the task, in order to ensure that they have 20 minutes rehearsal time. The psychologists will record the participants' physical language/non-verbal behaviours and then compare the results of the males with the results of the females in order to attempt to find a difference between each gender as regards non-verbal behaviour. The psychologists should record the participants' behaviour using event sampling. Types of non-verbal behaviour must be decided upon and categorised before the study i.e., crossing arms, hand gestures, shifting feet etc. Each time a participant displays one of these behaviours it would then be recorded on a recording sheet.

The reliability of the data collection could be established by using two psychologists to record and closely observe the data and then checking the inter-rater (observer) reliability between them. Inter-rater reliability determines the levels of concordance between each recorders' results and the higher the concordance rate the higher the reliability. A good level of inter-rater reliability is considered to be 80% and anything below this would therefore be considered to have low levels of reliability. Through comparing the separate recordings, we could ensure that we can make a statistical comparison of both raters.

Certain ethical considerations must also be taken into account. The participants must be aware of their right to withdraw, have given their informed consent to take part in the study and they must not be entirely deceived as to what the study is researching. These ethical considerations must be in place in order to protect the psychological welfare of the participants and to ensure that they are protected from physical and psychological harm during the study.

(300 words)

AQA A-LEVEL PSYCHOLOGY (7182/1)

PAPER 1

INTRODUCTORY TOPICS IN PSYCHOLOGY.

2017 (SECOND SET)

WEDNESDAY 7 JUNE 2017

AFTERNOON

TIME ALLOWED: 2 HOURS

SECTION A: SOCIAL INFLUENCE

Answer __all__ questions in this section (24 marks and 30 minutes for each section on Paper 1)

In an experiment, researchers arranged for participants to complete a very personal and embarrassing questionnaire in a room with other people. Each participant was tested individually. The other people were confederates of the experimenter.

In condition 1: the confederates completed the questionnaire.

In condition 2: the confederates refused to complete the questionnaire and asked to leave the experiment.

The researchers tested 15 participants in condition 1, and 15 different participants in condition 2.

The researchers recorded the number of participants who completed the questionnaire in each condition.

0 1 Identify the type of data in this experiment. Explain your answer.

[2 marks] (2.5 minutes) (AO2 = 2) (50 words maximum)

The type of data in this experiment is quantitative data. This is because the researchers counted the number of participants who completed the questionnaire in each condition i.e., conditions one and two and the data is numerical.

(37 words)

0 2 Using your knowledge of social influence, explain the likely outcome of this experiment.

[3 marks] (3.75 minutes) (AO2 = 3) (75 words maximum)

It is likely that more participants will complete the questionnaire in condition one than in condition two.

In condition one, the naive participant is likely to conform to the majority through normative social influence as the other confederates (the majority) completed the questionnaire.

However, the participants in condition two would be less likely to conform (and complete the questionnaire) as they have an ally (social support) of disobedient role models who support a non-conformist view.

(75 words)

For this study, the researchers had to use different participants in each condition and this could have affected the results.

0 3 Outline <u>one</u> way in which the researchers could have addressed this issue.

[4 marks] (5 minutes) (AO3 = 4) (100 words maximum)

One way in which the researchers could have addressed this issue is to randomly allocate participants to each condition by writing down all the names of the participants on slips of paper and then to put them in a hat. Then they must randomly withdraw 15 names and put them in condition 1 and then withdraw another 15 names and put them in condition 2. These will be the participants in condition 1 and condition 2 and should thus adequately address the issue above.

(84 words)

In order to analyse the difference in the number of participants who completed the questionnaire in each condition, the researchers used a chi-squared test.

0 4 Apart from reference to the level of measurement, give __two__ reasons why the researchers used the chi-squared test.

[2 marks] (2.5 minutes) (AO2 = 2) (50 words maximum)

The Chi-Squared test is suitable because the design is of independent groups with independent data – i.e., they were in either group 1 or group 2.

Furthermore, the Chi-Squared test is also suitable when researchers are looking for a difference or an association between two variables.

(45 words)

The calculated value of chi-squared in the experiment described on page 2 is __3.97__

Table 1: Critical values for the chi-squared test

Level of significance
df 0.1 0.05 0.02 0.01
1 2.71 3.84 5.41 6.64

The calculated value of chi-squared should be equal to or greater than the critical value to be statistically significant.

0 5 With reference to the critical values in __Table 1__, explain whether or not the calculated value of chi-squared is significant at the 5% level.

[2 marks] (2.5 minutes) (AO2 = 2) (50 words maximum)

The value of chi-squared is significant at the 5% level as the calculated (observed) value (3.97) is more than the critical table value of 3.84 at the 5% level.

(29 words)

0 6 Discuss the authoritarian personality as an explanation for obedience.

[8 marks] (10 minutes) (AO1 = 3; AO3 = 5) (200 words maximum)

An authoritarian personality is a collection of traits developed from overly strict parenting. An authoritarian personality is more likely to be conformist and obey and be servile towards people of perceived higher status and to be hostile towards those of perceived lower status. Adorno et al (1950) conducted a study of over 2000 participants using a questionnaire called the F-scale. This measured fascist tendencies, which is potentially at the core of the authoritarian personality.

(AO1 = 3)

Those with an authoritarian personality are generally more uncomfortable with uncertainty, and view everything as being either right or wrong, thus, demonstrating an inflexible attitude. There is also research support for the authoritarian personality as an explanation for obedience. Milgram (1963) found, when aiming to discern if there was a link between high levels of obedience and an authoritarian personality, that participants who were fully obedient in his study, scored higher on the F-scale in comparison to the disobedient participants. However, it is difficult to establish cause and effect between overly strict parenting and later levels of obedience. It is also difficult to easily account for obedience of entire social groups/societies. Furthermore, there may be individual differences that contribute to the development of the authoritarian personality.

(AO3 = 5)

(200 words)

0 7 Outline one alternative explanation for obedience.

[3 marks] (3.75 minutes) (AO1 = 3) (75 words maximum)

An alternative explanation for obedience is the agentic shift/state explanation. When a person acts independently this is called an autonomous state. The opposite of this is an agentic state, which occurs when an individual carries out the orders of an authority figure without thinking, with reduced moral accountability for their actions. To shift from autonomy to 'agency' is referred to as the 'agentic shift' and this is when a person experiences a diffusion of responsibility.

(75 words)

SECTION B: MEMORY

Answer __all__ questions in this section (24 marks and 30 minutes for each section on Paper 1)

Two types of long-term memory are procedural memory and episodic memory.

0 8 Explain __two__ differences between procedural memory and episodic memory.

[4 marks] (5 minutes) (AO3 = 4) (100 words maximum)

One difference between procedural memory and episodic memory is that procedural memories of actions, motor skills etc. have become 'automatic' and are unavailable for conscious inspection and difficult to explain verbally i.e., non-declarative. Whereas episodic memories, which include memories of personal experiences, can be expressed verbally i.e., they are declarative.

Another difference between procedural memory and episodic memory is that each type of memory may reside in a different area of the brain. Episodic memories are associated with the hippocampus whereas procedural memories are associated with the motor cortex. Procedural memories may also be more resistant to forgetting or amnesia.

(100 words)

In an investigation into memory, participants were presented with two different lists of words.

List A: Flip   Flit Flop Flap Flab Flan Flat
List B: Huge Large Great Giant Vast Mighty Epic

After seeing the lists, participants were tested on their ability to recall the words.

*When tested immediately, participants found it more difficult to recall the words from **List A** in the correct order.*

*When tested after 30 minutes, participants found it more difficult to recall the words from **List B** in the correct order.*

0 9 Using your knowledge of coding in memory, explain these findings.

[4 marks] (5 minutes) (AO2 = 4) (100 words maximum)

Immediate task – list A is made up of words that are acoustically similar and this will cause confusion (when tested immediately) as short-term memory (STM) uses acoustic, sound-based coding. This explains why participants found it difficult to recall the words in List A immediately after the presentation.

Delayed task – list B is made up of words that are semantically similar and this will cause confusion (when tested after 30 minutes) as recall in long-term memory (LTM) uses semantic, meaning-based coding. This explains why participants found it difficult to recall the words in List B after 30 minutes.

(99 words)

1 0 Outline and evaluate research (theories and/or studies) into the effects of misleading information on eyewitness testimony.

[16 marks] (20 minutes) (AO1=6; AO3 = 10) (400 words maximum)

Loftus and Palmer conducted studies into eyewitness testimony in 1974. They played a video of a car crash to participants and asked them 'how fast was the car going when it...the other car'. In different conditions they found that if they used the word 'smashed' the participants estimated an average speed of 41 miles per hour compared to an average estimation of 32 miles per hour if they used the word 'contacted'. A week later they also asked 'Did you see any broken glass?' using the word 'smashed' for one group, 'hit' for another and a third control group had no indication of speed given to them. The 'smashed' group had a higher number reporting 'broken glass', even though there was none.

(AO1 = 4)

In evaluating, we are aware that viewing a car crash on video is not as emotionally stimulating and produces less adrenaline than being in a real car crash and this may affect the results as it is also less ecologically valid. This demonstrates experimental reductionism also as the complex process of memory is reduced to the effect of the wording of a leading question on eyewitness memory. Therefore, their results do not reflect actual car accidents and we are unable to conclude if the effect of leading questions is ecologically valid in this context. The participants may have also guessed the aims of the experiment and thus displayed demand characteristics. However, both experiments also show that leading questions may have a long-term effect on eyewitness testimony.

(AO3 = 5)

Gabbert et al. (2003) investigated the effect of post-event discussion. Her participants watched a video of a girl stealing money. Participants in the co-witness group were told that they had watched the same video; however, they had seen different perspectives.

(AO1 = 2)

In evaluating, 71% of the witnesses in the co-witness group recalled information they had not seen, despite the fact that they had not seen her commit a crime. This could be the result of poor memory, where people assimilate new information into personalised accounts of the event and are unable to distinguish between what they have seen and what they have heard. However, paired discussions could have clearly influenced the recall of crime and co-witnesses mixing may have led to misinformation, memory contamination and memory conformity. Witnesses may have clearly conformed with others to receive social approval.

Further research is required to demonstrate the exact effects of misleading information on eyewitness testimony.

(AO3 = 5)

(400 words)

SECTION C: ATTACHMENT

Answer <u>all</u> questions in this section (24 marks and 30 minutes for each section on Paper 1)

Answer <u>all</u> questions in this section

1 1 Which <u>two</u> of the following are associated with an insecure-resistant attachment type? Choose <u>two</u> from the options <u>A, B, C, D</u> and <u>E.</u>

[2 marks] (2.5 minutes) (AO1 = 2)

A Extreme stranger anxiety
B Indifference when the mother leaves the room
C Low willingness to explore the new environment
D Moderate levels of separation anxiety
E Obvious joy when reunited with the mother

A
C

1 2 Name <u>three</u> of the stages of attachment identified by Schaffer.

[3 marks] (3.75 minutes) (AO1 = 3)

Pre-Attachment (asocial)
Indiscriminate (diffuse)
Discriminate (specific)

1 3 What is meant by 'reciprocity' in the context of caregiver-infant interaction?

[2 marks] (2.5 minutes) (AO1 = 2) (50 words maximum)

In the context of caregiver-infant interactions, reciprocity is a two-way/mutual process; each party responds to the other's signals to sustain interaction through turn-taking. There is interactional synchrony as infant and adult react and respond in time to sustain communication and thus elicit a response from the other.

(47 words)

1 4 Briefly evaluate research into caregiver-infant interaction.

[4 marks] (5 minutes) (AO3 = 4) (100 words maximum)

There is the possibility of observer bias, as often the researchers are also the main observers. Investigator effects can be nullified however by having two researchers assess the caregiver-infant interaction and by comparing their scores to see if they match or are similar. This is known as inter-rater/observer reliability.

Another issue that researchers might encounter when investigating caregiver-infant interactions is the issue of extraneous variables affecting the results. Well-controlled studies, however, capture micro-sequences of interaction and look to ameliorate the issues of extraneous variables of intentionality in caregiver-infant interaction by discerning if imitative behaviours are deliberate or conscious, for example.

(100 words)

Anca is an orphan who has recently been adopted by a British couple. Before being adopted, Anca lived in an institution with lots of other children in very poor conditions. Her new parents are understandably concerned about how Anca's early experiences may affect her in the future.

1 5 Use your knowledge of the effects of institutionalisation to advise Anca's new parents about what to expect.

[5 marks] (6.25 minutes) (AO2 = 5) (125 words maximum)

Institutionalisation can have effects on physical, intellectual, social and emotional development. Anca's parents could be advised to expect that Anca may display signs of Type D 'disinhibited attachment' and Anca may not know how to behave towards strangers.

Another effect could be delayed intellectual development, low IQ problems and difficulty concentrating. Anca may therefore struggle more at school than others in her peer group and may not learn new behaviours and concepts at the same rate.

In terms of her emotional development, Anca may experience more temper tantrums. However, if Anca was adopted before the age of 6 months, the effects may not be as severe and long term as if had she been adopted later. The effects may also be reversed with sensitive parenting.

(125 words)

1 6 Discuss findings of research into cultural variations in attachment.

[8 marks] (10 minutes) (AO1 = 3; AO3 = 5) (200 words maximum)

Van Ijzendoorn and Kroonenberg's research into cultural variations in attachment found that secure attachment was the most common type of attachment in all cultures. Japan and Israel displayed higher levels of insecure-resistant attachment (collectivist cultures) which was supported by Sagi et al (1991) who found high rates of insecure-resistant attachments in Israeli children. Germany (an individualistic culture) showed higher levels of insecure-avoidant attachment. Van Ijzendoorn and Kroonenberg concluded that secure attachment is the type of attachment that is best for healthy development.

(AO1 = 3)

Meta-analyses include very large samples and thus increase the validity of the findings. One issue, however, with Van Ijzendoorn and Kroonenberg's research is that the underlying methodology of the studies in their meta-analysis used the 'strange situation'. They also reported significant differences in the distribution of attachment types in different cultures. For example, Germany had the highest rate of insecure-avoidant attachment which may be the result of different childrearing practices and not a more 'insecure' population. Consequently, the underlying methodology used in their analysis may be biased towards American/British cultures and samples in studies may not represent the culture as a whole. Cultural variations may also be due to an interaction of nature and nurture.

(AO3 = 5)

(197 words)

SECTION D: PSYCHOPATHOLOGY

Answer __all__ questions in this section (24 marks and 30 minutes for each section on Paper 1)

1 7 Which __two__ of the following are cognitive characteristics of obsessive-compulsive disorder (OCD)?

Choose __two__ from the options __A__, __B__, __C__, __D__ and __E__.

[2 marks] (2.5 minutes) (AO1 = 2)

A Awareness that behaviour is irrational
B Compulsions
C Disgust
D High anxiety
E Obsessions

A
E

1 8 Outline one or more ways in which behaviourists treat phobias.

[6 marks] (7.5 minutes) (AO1 = 6) (150 words maximum)

Systematic desensitisation is based on classical conditioning and uses counter-conditioning to help patients unlearn their phobias, by eliciting another response; relaxation instead of fear. A patient works with their therapist to create a fear hierarchy, ranking phobic situations from least to most terrifying. After the formation of the anxiety hierarchy, the patient is taught relaxation techniques such as deep breathing. The therapist then gradually works up a patients fear hierarchy until the patient is able to maintain a relaxed state when confronted with the situation that triggers their phobia the most, such as holding a spider if arachnophobic. The patient then no longer associates the stimulus with danger and thus anxiety. Two emotional states (fear and relaxation) cannot coexist at the same time, (a theory known as reciprocal inhibition) and eventually relaxation will replace the fear. Gradual exposure then leads to eventual extinction of the fear of the phobic stimulus.

(150 words)

Rob is a sixth form student who has started hearing voices in his head. The voices come often, are usually threatening and make Rob feel frightened. The voices are making it difficult for Rob to complete his homework properly and he is worried about how this may affect his chances of going to university. Rob has not told anyone about his experiences, but his parents and teachers have noticed that he appears distracted, anxious and untidy.

1 9 Outline and evaluate failure to function adequately __and__ deviation from ideal mental health as definitions of abnormality. Refer to the experiences of Rob in your answer.

[16 marks] (20 minutes) (AO1 = 6; AO2 = 4; A03 = 6) (400 words maximum)

According to the failure to function adequately definition, abnormality is judged as an inability to deal with the demands of everyday living and to live independently in society. A person's behaviour is maladaptive, irrational or dangerous and causes personal distress and distress to others. Rob could be considered abnormal as there is evidence that Rob is not coping with everyday tasks, finding it difficult to 'complete his homework' and he is 'untidy'. Rob has personal distress i.e.; feelings of anxiety and he is 'frightened' and his symptoms are also causing distress as 'his parents and teachers' have noticed his anxiety.

(AO1 = 3; AO2 = 2)

The failure to function adequately definition recognises the patient's perspective and judging a person, in this case, Rob, as distressed or distressing relies on subjective assessment. It is therefore, a useful tool for assessing psychopathological behaviour. However, not all abnormal behaviour is associated with distress and a failure to cope i.e., psychopathy, and not all maladaptive behaviour is an indicator of mental illness. There is also the issue of individual differences, for example, one person who hears voices may be unable to function adequately; whereas, another person may suffer from the same symptoms, but function; thus, questioning the validity of this definition.

(AO3 = 3)

Deviation from ideal mental health is another definition of abnormality whereby the absence of signs of mental health is used to judge abnormality. Jahoda (1958) outlined a series of principles, including: accurate perception of reality, resistance to stress; positive attitude towards self; autonomy/independence; environmental mastery and self-actualisation. It could be argued that Rob does not have an accurate view of reality as he is 'hearing voices'. The voices are also potentially preventing Rob from fulfilling his potential and achieving self-actualisation and 'may affect his chances of going to university.' According to this definition, the more criteria someone fails to meet, the more abnormal they are.

(AO1 = 3; AO2 = 2)

Jahoda's definition takes a positive, holistic approach to diagnosis. However, the criteria for mental health are arguably too demanding and unrealistic. There is some correlation with deviation from social norms as a definition of abnormality which outlines an individual who contrasts with the behaviours of their society (the social norms) and deviation from statistical norms which is behaviour that is rare statistically and is considered abnormal. There is cultural bias also in some of Jahoda's criteria, i.e., the value placed on independence and autonomy could be considered to be culturally relative and biased.

(AO3 = 3)

(400 words)

AQA A-LEVEL PSYCHOLOGY (7182/2)

PAPER 2

PSYCHOLOGY IN CONTEXT

2017 (SECOND SET)

WEDNESDAY 14 JUNE 2017

AFTERNOON

TIME ALLOWED: 2 HOURS

SECTION A: APPROACHES IN PSYCHOLOGY

*Answer **all** questions in this section (24 marks and 30 minutes for this section)*

A recent study showed that Alzheimer's disease may be partly inherited.

John's father suffered from Alzheimer's disease. John is keen to get genetically tested to see if he will develop Alzheimer's disease.

*0 1 Explain why John's genotype will **not** reveal whether he will suffer from Alzheimer's disease.*

[4 marks] (5 minutes) (AO2 = 4) (100 words maximum)

The genetic test reveals the genotype and not the phenotype. John's genotype will only reveal his set of genes and not their interaction with the environment. A genetic test will only reveal if he is predisposed to suffering from Alzheimer's disease but it will not reveal whether he will develop or suffer from the disorder at a later stage of his life. Environmental factors may also contribute to the disorder as developing Alzheimer's disease depends on an interaction between inherited factors and the environment. As mentioned above, the results of the study suggest that Alzheimer's disease is only partly inherited.

(100 words)

0 2 Describe the structure of the personality according to the psychodynamic approach.

[4 marks] (5 minutes) (AO1 = 4) (100 words maximum)

According to Freud, personality has three components; the id, ego and superego.

The id (instinctive/internal drive) focuses on the self, is irrational and emotional, (dealing principally with feelings and needs) and seeks hedonistic pleasure (pleasure principle). It is believed to be formed in the first 18 months from birth.

The ego is rational, balancing the id and the superego, ('reality principle'). It is formed between 18 months to 3 years of age.

The superego ('morality principle'), acts as the conscience or a moral guide and is based on parental and societal values. It is formed between 3-6 years of age.

(100 words)

Tatiana's parents are concerned about her mobile phone use. She is an anxious child and has low self-esteem. Tatiana only feels good about herself when she receives messages or positive comments on social media. She feels safe when she has her phone and socially isolated without it.

Tatiana's parents worry that her dependence on her mobile phone is starting to affect her well-being and achievement at school.

0 3 Outline and evaluate the humanistic approach. Refer to Tatiana's behaviour in your answer.

[16 marks] (20 minutes) (AO1 = 6; AO2 = 4; AO3 = 6) (400 words maximum)

Humanistic psychology, focusses on the work of Maslow and Rogers. Maslow's hierarchy of needs (1943) states that the most basic needs are biological needs i.e., food, water, clothing, shelter, sleep; safety needs, which include resources and health; next is the need for love and belonging, from friends and family and then there is the need for esteem. Both self-esteem and respect from others provides motivation to progress through the hierarchy to self-actualisation.

Tatiana requires her mobile phone to meet her safety needs i.e., 'feels safe when she has her phone'. Her love and belonging needs may be affected when she feels 'socially isolated without it', which could link to her not meeting her self-esteem needs, and thus inhibit her self-actualisation i.e., affecting her 'achievement at school'.

(AO1 = 3; AO2 = 2)

Rogers was primarily interested in two needs: the need for self-worth and the need for unconditional positive regard from other people. Rogers' focused also on the concept of self and self-acceptance. For Rogers, unhappiness and dissatisfaction were the outcomes of a psychological gap between self-concept and the ideal self. Tatiana may be experiencing a gap between her self-concept i.e., 'low self-esteem' and anxiety and her ideal self when she 'feels good about herself when she receives messages or comments'. Incongruence between self-concept and the ideal self leads to negative feelings of self-worth. Her conditions of worth are potentially linked to feeling the need to text friends and use social media for acceptance and friendship as she does not receive unconditional positive regard from others.

(AO1 = 3; AO2 = 2)

The humanistic approach has limited application due to its abstract concepts. Concepts within the hierarchy of needs (e.g., self-actualisation) are difficult to operationalise and therefore very difficult to test empirically. The humanistic approach therefore lacks empirical evidence to support its claims. Humanistic psychology does not use nomothetic methods of investigation. Consequently, psychologists are unable to provide research support for the existence of the hierarchy of needs and other aspects of humanistic psychology making such theories and concepts questionable. However, the humanistic approach is not reductionist which may improve validity.

It has had a major influence on psychological counselling. For example, many contemporary therapists use Rogers' person centred counselling techniques. This means it has temporal validity and real–world applications. However, some critics argue that the humanistic approach offers an unrealistic view of human nature and there are arguments as to whether behaviour is largely due to free will or environmental/deterministic factors.

(AO3 = 6)

(400 words)

SECTION B: BIOPSYCHOLOGY

Answer <u>all</u> questions in this section (24 marks and 30 minutes for this section)

0 4 Explain the process of synaptic transmission.

[4 marks] (5 minutes) (AO1 = 4) (100 words maximum)

Synaptic transmission is a process whereby a nerve impulse passes across the synaptic gap from the presynaptic neuron to the post-synaptic neuron. Information is passed down the axon of the neuron as electrical impulses (action potentials) and reaches the presynaptic terminal by crossing over the synaptic gap. Electrical impulses trigger the release of chemical messengers, known as neurotransmitters. They cross the synapse from vesicles and combine with receptors on the postsynaptic membrane. The stimulation of postsynaptic receptors by neurotransmitters results in either excitation (depolarisation) or inhibition (hyperpolarisation) of the postsynaptic membrane; making the cell more or less likely to fire.

(100 words)

Lotta's grandmother suffered a stroke to the left hemisphere, damaging Broca's area and the motor cortex.

0 5 Using your knowledge of the functions of Broca's area and the motor cortex, describe the problems that Lotta's grandmother is likely to experience.

[4 marks] (5 minutes) (AO2 = 4) (100 words maximum)

As a result of damage to Broca's area, Lotta's grandmother is likely to suffer from language and speech problems (Broca's aphasia). Lotta's grandmother will only be able to iterate in short meaningful sentences which will take considerable effort. Her speech will also lack fluency and there will be difficulty with certain words.

As a consequence of damage to the motor cortex, Lotta's grandmother is likely to suffer from loss of muscle function and paralysis and motor impairments on the right side of her body as the left motor regions are responsible for movement on the right side of the body.

(100 words)

Lotta worries that because of her grandmother's age she will not be able to make any recovery.

0 6 Using your knowledge of plasticity and functional recovery of the brain after trauma, explain why Lotta might be wrong.

[4 marks] (5 minutes) (AO2 = 4) (100 words maximum)

Lotta's grandmother might still be capable of functional recovery through brain plasticity. Plasticity allows the brain to cope better with the indirect effects of brain damage following a stroke. There can be an increased brain stimulation of the opposite hemisphere and physiotherapy may enhance Lotta's grandmother's recovery. Studies on plasticity also suggest that women recover quicker than men.

Functional compensation can also occur through other undamaged areas of the brain and although Lotta's grandmother is older, her brain might still be able to form new connections (axons and dendrites) between neurons and thereby reduce the severity of Lotta's grandmother's impairment.

(100 words)

A researcher wants to investigate the effectiveness of physiotherapy in the recovery of stroke patients with brain damage. Carers of stroke patients will be sent questionnaires to produce quantitative data.

0 7 Explain one disadvantage of obtaining quantitative data in this study.

[2 marks] (2.5 minutes) (AO2 = 2) (50 words maximum)

Quantitative data lacks detail, (unlike qualitative data) which may decrease the validity of the findings. For example, when carers rate a patient's improvement through questionnaires, the quantitative data obtained does not provide an insight into how and why they find the therapy effective, which may be more useful to psychologists.

(50 words)

0 8 Write one question that could be used in the researcher's questionnaire to produce quantitative data and one question that could be used in the researcher's questionnaire to produce qualitative data.

[2 marks] (2.5 minutes) (AO2 = 2) (50 words maximum)

Quantitative data question: 'On average how many hours of physiotherapy does the patient receive per week?'

Qualitative data question: 'How does physiotherapy help your patients with their brain damage?'

(29 words)

0 9 Outline and evaluate <u>one or more</u> ways of studying the brain.

[8 marks] (10 minutes) (AO1 = 3; AO3 = 5) (200 words maximum)

Functional magnetic resonance imaging (fMRI) is a brain-scanning technique that uses magnetic field and radio waves to monitor blood flow. It measures the change in the energy released by haemoglobin, reflecting the activity of the brain and its oxygen consumption to give a fluid picture of the brain. Thus, activity in regions of interest in the brain can be compared during a base line task and during a specific activity.

An electroencephalogram (EEG) – uses electrodes which are put on the scalp and detect neuronal activity directly below where they are placed and differing numbers of electrodes can be used depending on focus of the research.

Functional magnetic resonance imaging (fMRI) captures dynamic brain activity yet interpretation of fMRI is a complex process and is affected by temporal resolution, biased interpretation and by the baseline task used. fMRI research is also expensive, leading to reduced sample sizes which negatively impacts the validity of the research.

Using an electroencephalogram (EEGs) is cheaper so it can be more widely used in research yet EEGs have poor spatial resolution. There are also advantages of investigating brain activity in humans rather than generalising from animal lesion and single electrode recording studies, in terms of validity.

[200 words]

SECTION C: RESEARCH METHODS

Answer <u>all</u> questions in this section (48 marks and 60 minutes for this section)

A psychologist wanted to test whether listening to music improves running performance.

The psychologist conducted a study using 10 volunteers from a local gym. The psychologist used a repeated measures design. Half of the participants were assigned to condition A (without music) and half to condition B (with music).

All participants were asked to run 400 metres as fast as they could on a treadmill in the psychology department. All participants were given standardised instructions. All participants wore headphones in both conditions. The psychologist recorded their running times in seconds. The participants returned to the psychology department the following week and repeated the test in the other condition.

1 0 Identify the type of experiment used in this study. Shade <u>one</u> box only.

A Laboratory
B Natural
C Quasi
D Research

[1 mark] (1.25 minutes) (AO2 = 1)

A

1 1 Identify the operationalised dependent variable in this study.

[2 marks] (2.5 minutes) (AO2 = 2) (50 words maximum)

The operationalised dependent variable would be the time taken to run 400 metres in seconds.

(15 words)

The results of the study are given in Table 1 below.

Table 1 Mean number of seconds taken to complete the 400m run and the standard deviation for both conditions

	Condition A (without music)	Condition B (with music)
Mean 400m time (s)	123	117
Standard deviation	9.97	14.5

1 2 Explain why a histogram would <u>not</u> be an appropriate way of displaying the means shown in Table 1.

[2 marks] (2.5 minutes) (AO2 = 2) (50 words maximum)

A histogram would not be appropriate because you need to have continuous data or scores for each participant in order to draw a histogram. The data is categorical (with music or without music) and the data represents two separate conditions, therefore a bar chart would be appropriate for this experiment.

(50 words)

1 3 Name a more appropriate graph to display the means shown in Table 1. Suggest appropriate X (horizontal) and Y (vertical) axis labels for your graph choice.

[3 marks] (3.75 minutes) (AO3 = 3) (75 words maximum)

An appropriate graph is a bar chart.
An appropriate X-axis label would be 'With or without music'.
An appropriate Y-axis label would be the 'Mean/average number of seconds taken to complete the 400-metre run'.

(34 words)

1 4 What do the mean and standard deviation values in Table 1 suggest about the participants' performances with and without music? Justify your answer.

[4 marks] (5 minutes) (AO2 = 2; AO3 = 2) (100 words maximum)

The mean times suggest that listening to music while running 400 metres improves performance as shown through the difference in the mean scores in each condition. For example, the mean time taken when listening to music in Condition B was 117 seconds in comparison to 123 seconds for Condition A.

Standard deviation reveals the variation or consistency in the sets of scores in each condition. There is a clear difference between the standard deviations in each condition. In Condition B listening to music has a more varied effect on running performance because the SD was 4.53 higher than Condition A.

(100 words)

1 5 Calculate the percentage decrease in the mean time it took participants to run 400 metres when listening to music. Show your workings. Give your answer to three significant figures.

[4 marks] (5 minutes) (AO2 = 4)

123 – 117 = 6

6 / 123 = 0.048780

0.048780 x 100 = 4.878

= 4.88

1 6 The researcher used a directional hypothesis and analysed the data using a related t-test. The calculated value of t where degrees of freedom (df) = 9 was 1.4377. He decided to use the 5% level of significance.

Table 2 Table of critical values of t
Level of significance for a one tailed test
Level of significance for a two tailed test

	one-t 0.05	0.025
two-t	0.10	0.05
df = 1	6.314	12.706
2	2.920	4.303
3	2.353	3.182
4	2.132	2.776
5	2.015	2.571
6	1.943	2.447
7	1.895	2.365
8	1.860	2.306
9	1.833	2.262
10	1.812	2.228

Calculated value of t must be equal to or greater than the critical value in this table for significance to be shown.

Give __three__ reasons why the researcher used a related t-test in this study and, using Table 2, explain whether or not the results are significant.

[5 marks] (6.25 minutes) (AO2 = 5) (125 words maximum)

A t-test is an appropriate choice of test for this data because a difference between the two sets of data is predicted. The data is of an interval/ratio level as the researchers recorded the time taken to run the 400m in seconds. A repeated measures design has been used as each participant took part in both conditions.

The result is not significant (at the 5% level) because the calculated value of t (1.4377) is less than the critical table value of t, which is 1.833 (at 0.05, for a directional hypothesis where df is 9) thus accepting the null hypothesis.

(100 words)

1 7 What is meant by a Type II error? Explain why psychologists normally use the 5% level of significance in their research.

[3 marks] (3.75 minutes) (AO1 = 3) (75 words maximum)

A Type II error occurs when a significant difference in the data is overlooked as it is wrongly accepted as being not significant, thus accepting the null hypothesis in error (a false negative).

Psychologists normally use a 5% significance level, as this is considered an acceptable level at which to claim significant results. Thus, the psychologists are 95% confident that their results are due to the independent variable having an effect on the dependent variable.

(75 words)

1 8 Identify <u>one</u> extraneous variable that could have affected the results of this study.

Suggest why it would have been important to control this extraneous variable and how it could have been controlled in this study.

[3 marks] (3.75 minutes) (AO2 = 2; AO3 = 1) (75 words maximum)

One extraneous variable that could have affected the results is an environmental variable, i.e., the time of day that the participants completed their 400m run.
It is important to control this extraneous variable as it could impact the dependent variable. Therefore, the participants could complete both conditions at approximately the same time of day to ensure control of this variable and ensure that the time of day does not affect the validity of the results.

(75 words)

The report was submitted for peer review and a number of recommendations were advised.

Describe the process and purposes of peer review.

[6 marks] (7.5 minutes) (AO1 = 6) (150 words maximum)

Peer review is a part of the scientific process whereby other psychologists working in a similar field, provide independent scrutiny of a research report in terms of its validity, significance and originality. Research reports are submitted to a panel and assessed before they decide whether it can be published. Reviewers can accept the manuscript as it is, accept it with revisions, suggest that the author makes revisions and re-submits or reject it fully without providing the possibility of re-submission. An editor makes the final decision as to whether to accept or reject the research report based on the reviewers' comments and/or recommendations.

The purposes of peer review are to ensure the quality and relevance of the research, e.g., in methodology, data analysis etc. and to ensure the accuracy of the findings and to evaluate the proposed designs (in terms of aims, quality and value of the research) for research funding.

(150 words)

People's perception of how they spend their time at the gym is often not very accurate. Some spend more time chatting than on the treadmill. A psychologist decides to observe the actual behaviour of an opportunity sample of gym users at a local gym.

2 0 Explain why it is more appropriate for the psychologist to use an observation than a questionnaire in this case.

[3 marks] (3.75 minutes) (AO2 = 3) (75 words maximum)

An observation is more appropriate because a self-report method i.e., a questionnaire, could lead to socially desirable answers as people may present themselves in the best possible light. Observations allow researchers to assess behaviour directly as the researcher is collecting primary data and does not rely on participants reporting their own behaviour. This improves the validity of the data gathered and it is an accurate reflection of how people spend their time at the gym.

(75 words)

Design an observational study to investigate how people spend their time at the gym. In your answer you will be awarded credit for providing appropriate details of:

• type of observation with justification
• operationalised behavioural categories
• use of time and/or event sampling with justification
• how reliability of data collection could be assessed.

[12 marks] (15 minutes) (AO2 = 6; AO3 = 6) (300 words maximum)

The type of observation I would conduct would be a covert, naturalistic observation of an opportunity sample. This would ensure that the behaviour I am observing is natural and that observer bias is minimised. There are no ethical issues also as behaviour is taking place in a public setting and naturalistic observations tend to have higher external validity.

I would conduct a structured observation, in one set part of the gym. Two specific and observable behaviours I would record would include two specific categories; when people rest (either standing or seated) and the number of times interaction occurs with another gym member (event sampling as the behaviour occurs). These would be my operationalised behavioural categories.

I would collect this data using a tally sheet and the number of gym users engaging in each activity would be recorded specifically at five-minute time intervals (time sampling). Time sampling would be appropriate as it would allow us to gain a snapshot of each activity and record what different gym users are doing at five-minute time intervals and allow us to see whether people rest or interact with others at pre-determined intervals.

I would establish the reliability of the data collection by using two observers/raters and comparing separate recordings, to check for inter-rater/observer reliability. The reliability of the data could then be assessed through statistical comparison (correlation) of the data from both observers/raters, leading to intra-observer reliability. Thus, having operationalised the behavioural categories clearly and trained the observers in how to use the tally sheet to record behaviour, I will get them to observe the same gym for one hour and use a correlation test to determine how similar their scores were for each behaviour. If I find a correlation coefficient of 80% or more, this would indicate a good level of inter-rater/observer reliability.

(300 words)

ASSESSMENT OBJECTIVES.

There are three assessment objectives assessed in each examination: **AO1, AO2** and **AO3.**

AO1 = Outline. This involves outlining your knowledge and understanding. It involves recalling and describing theories, studies and methods.

AO2 = Apply. This involves applying your knowledge and understanding. You must apply your knowledge to different situations and contexts. You will apply this from the information given in the text provided in the question; which will be a theoretical or practical example.

AO3 = Evaluate. This involves analysing and interpreting. Evaluating studies and theories or drawing conclusions.

There may be one, two or all (only in the extended writing questions) of the assessment objectives in each question. Therefore, it is vitally important to be aware of the structure of how the assessment objectives are allocated in each question of the exam in order to maximise your opportunities to obtain full marks in each question.

It is worth noting that **the Assessment Objectives that are to be met for each question are not provided in the examination itself**, which provides a further complication for you. However, I have provided which assessment objectives are being assessed in the practice questions in this book to give you more awareness of what each type of question is looking for in the answer.

<u>Additional points to remember.</u>

1) When you are answering the A02 application section of the question, it is sometimes useful to write 'In terms of application' before providing your AO2 points and give a quotation if possible, particularly if the question is asking you to 'refer' back to the information provided. Also, when you are answering the A03 evaluation section of the question, it is sometimes useful to write 'In terms of evaluation' before providing your AO3 points.

2) Generally, my students prefer to separate the AO's out in their answers i.e., for a 12 mark (AO1 = 6; A03 =6) answer they will write 2 paragraphs with the first paragraph being AO1 (6 marks) and then the second paragraph being AO3 (6 marks) or 4 alternating AO1 and AO3 paragraphs with 3 marks of AO1 or AO3 in each paragraph.

TIMINGS.

Please allocate minutes per mark! In the Psychology AQA A level examination Papers 1 and 2; there are 96 marks to aim for in 120 minutes; which works out at **1.25 minutes per mark**. (This is the same minutes per mark as in all your AS and A level Papers). Therefore, **if a question is worth 8 marks then you would spend roughly 10 minutes** on this question. In the examples in this book, I have given you the maximum amount of time allowed for each question which always works out at **1.25 minutes per mark.**

A good rule of thumb is to apply the principle that you get **1 mark per correct point made in your answer** i.e., 4 good points for a 4-mark question. My students find that 1 mark per sentence also helps them to apply this rule generally. Similar to all the principles in this book, **you must apply and follow the correct timings for each question and stick to them throughout your exam to get an A or A star in your Psychology examinations.**

If you have extra time allocated to you, just change the calculation to accommodate the extra time you have for each mark i.e., approximately 1.5 minutes per mark if you have 25% extra time and 1.8 minutes per mark if you have 50% extra time. Allocate within your time management the time for checking if you wish but **move on from the set question as soon as you have reached or are coming towards your time limit**. This ensures that you have excellent coverage of your whole exam and therefore attain a very good mark.

Without applying this principle in these examinations (and to a large extent all examinations) you cannot achieve the highest marks! **Apply all of the principles provided in this book to succeed**!

Additional points to remember.

1) **10% of your examination will be composed of mathematical questions**. But please do not be overly concerned, it is only GCSE level Mathematics and involves basic arithmetic, data and graphs.

2) **Approximately a third of all questions at AS and A level Psychology will involve Research Methods** and they can occur in any paper or section of your examination, not just in the Research Methods section. **Please make sure you apply a strong focus to Research Methods in your revision** and remember again that the Mathematics involved is only set at a GCSE level of difficulty.

APPROXIMATE WORD COUNT PER MARK IN PSYCHOLOGY.

Now that you know what is on each examination, how the assessment objectives are assessed and the time allocated for each type of question we come to what would be considered the correct word count per mark for each question. The primary principle though is to spend the right amount of time on each question as mentioned on the previous pages.

Unfortunately, there is no exact rule here as some questions are mathematical and do not require words whilst extended writing questions and essays tend to follow the set word count below more exactly.

In the answers in this book, I have provided the maximum word count for each answer which works out at **25 words per mark**. However, a good rule of thumb is between **15 and 25 words**.

15 words per mark - minimum word count.

20 words per mark – a generally good word count per mark.

25 words per mark – **The maximum word count generally able to be produced, in the time allocated.**

<u>Additional points to remember.</u>

1) If your answer has quality, 25 words per mark gives you the best chance of obtaining the highest marks in your Psychology exam. Obviously, it does not if you are waffling however. (Please remember to answer the question set and to move on in the time allocated.)

2) Generally, Research Methods questions tend to need less words per mark but there are exceptions to this rule.

3) Remember: **Apply the principle that you get 1 mark per correct point made in your answer and 1 mark per sentence also helps to apply this rule** and if you are concise you can obtain each mark in 15 words of writing. I am aware that some students can write faster than others but all should be able to write 15 words per mark at A level in 1.25 minutes (if they have not been allocated extra time). This is where conciseness is important. However, using the principle of one point per sentence: **Each point/sentence and therefore mark should generally be between 15 and 25 words and completed in 1.25 minutes.**

4) My students have applied all the techniques I am providing you with to gain A's and A stars in their Psychology examinations. You can replicate them by following the advice in this book.

Thank you for purchasing this book,

Very best wishes for your examinations!

Joseph

AUTHOR'S NOTE.

This book will provide you with crystal clear and accurate examples of 'A' star grade AQA A level Paper 1 and Paper 2 Psychology examinations from the new syllabus and enables students to achieve the same grade in their upcoming examinations.

I teach both GCSE and A level Psychology and I am a qualified and experienced Psychology teacher and tutor of over 17 years standing. I teach, write and provide independent tuition in Central and West London.

The resources in this book WILL help you get an A or A star in your AQA A level Psychology examinations, as they have done and will continue to do so, for my students.

Best wishes,

Joseph

ABOUT THE AUTHOR.

I graduated from the Universities of Liverpool and Leeds and I obtained first class honours in my teacher training.

I have taught and provided private tuition for over 17 years up to University level. I also write academic resources for the Times Educational Supplement.

My tuition students have been fortunate enough to attain places to study at Oxford, Cambridge and Imperial College, London and other Russell Group Universities. The students have done very well in their examinations and one Psychology student even obtained full UMS marks in her A2 Psychology examination. I hope and know that my Psychology books can enable you to take the next step on your academic journey.

Printed in Great Britain
by Amazon